# *More* european madrigals

## FOR MIXED VOICES

EDITED BY

# egon kraus

English Words by
MARIA PELIKAN

ED-2777

ISBN 978-0-7935-5703-5

## G. SCHIRMER, Inc.

# Ride la primavera
## Spring Has Arrived

Heinrich Schütz
1585-1672

ra, tor - na la bel - la Clo - ri, o - di la ron-di -
land bring-ing the love-ly Clo - ri, Hear the re-joic-ing
bel - la Clo - ri, o - di la ron-di - nel -
love- ly Clo - ri, Hear the re- joic-ing swal -
tor - na la bel - la Clo - ri,
bring-ing the love - ly Clo - ri,
8 tor - na la bel - la Clo - ri,
bring-ing the love - ly Clo - ri,

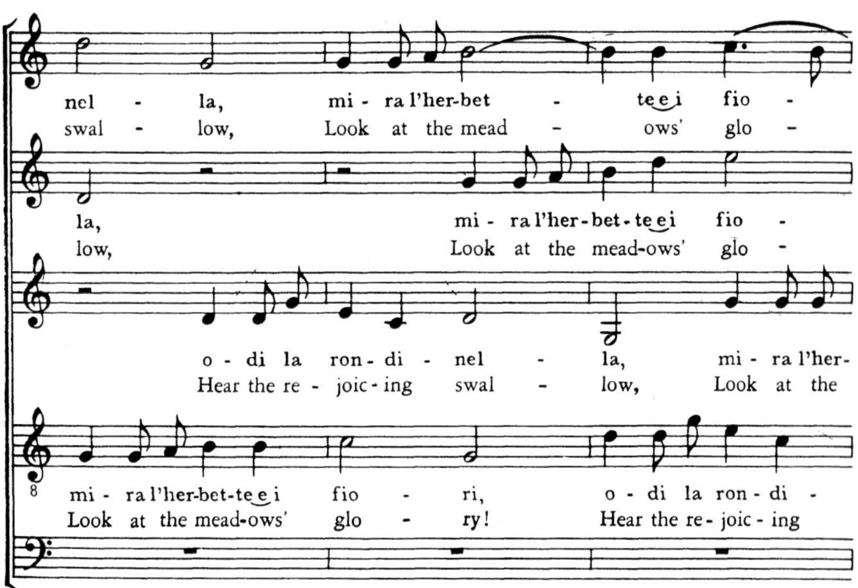
nel - la, mi - ra l'her-bet - te e i fio -
swal - low, Look at the mead - ows' glo -
la, mi - ra l'her-bet-te e i fio -
low, Look at the mead-ows' glo -
o - di la ron - di - nel - la, mi - ra l'her-
Hear the re - joic-ing swal - low, Look at the
8 mi - ra l'her-bet-te e i fio - ri, o - di la ron - di -
Look at the mead-ows' glo - ry! Hear the re - joic - ing

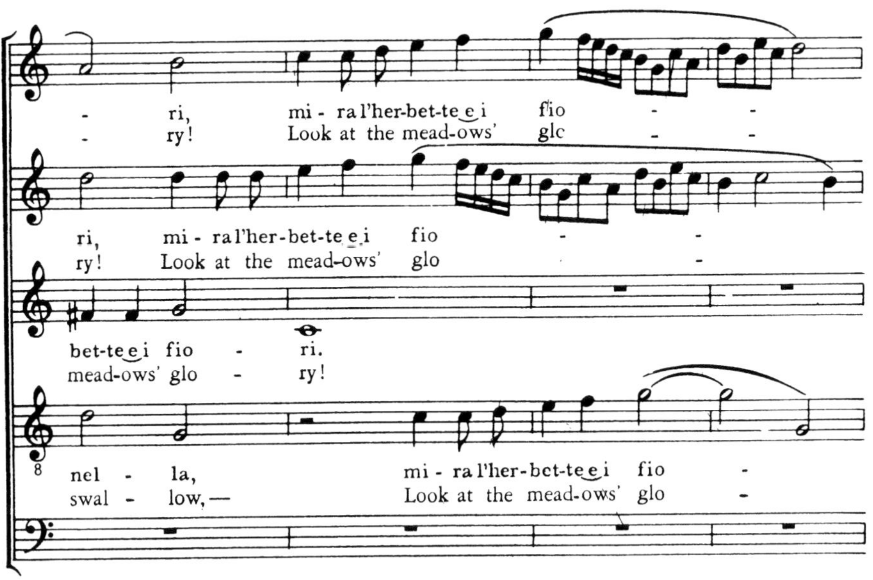
- ri, mi - ra l'her-bet-te e i fio - -
- ry! Look at the mead-ows' glc - -
ri, mi - ra l'her-bet-te e i fio - - -
ry! Look at the mead-ows' glo -
bet-te e i fio - ri.
mead-ows' glo - ry!
nel - la, mi - ra l'her-bet-te e i fio -
swal - low,— Look at the mead-ows' glo -

ri. Ma, ma tu Clo -
ry! Ah, but my Clo -
ri. Ma tu Clo - ri più
ry! Ah, my Clo - ri is
Ma, ma tu Clo - ri più bel -
Ah, ah my Clo - ri is fair -
ri. Ma, ma tu Clo -
ry! Ah, ah my Clo -
Ma, tu Clo -
Ah, my Clo -

ri
ri
più bel
is fair
bel - la, più bel
fair - er, is fair
- la, più bel - - la, più
- er, is fair - - er, is
ri più bel - la, più bel
ri is fair - er, is fair
ri
ri
più bel
is fair
la, più bel - - la
er, is fair - - er,
la, più bel - - la
er, is fair - - er,
bel - la, più bel - la
fair - er, is fair - er,
la, più bel - - la
er, is fair - - er,
la, più bel - - - la
er, is fair - - - er,

nel - la sta - gion no - vel - la, nel - la sta -
than the un - fold - ing sea - son; than the un -
nel - la sta - gion no - vel - la, nel - la sta -
than the un - fold - ing sea - son; than the un -
nel - la sta -
than the un -
nel - la sta - gion no - vel - la, nel - la sta -
than the un - fold - ing sea - son; than the un -
nel - la sta -
than the un -

gion no - vel - la
fold - ing sea - son;
gion no - vel - la
fold - ing sea - son;
gion no - vel - la
fold - ing sea - son;
gion no - vel - la ser - bi l'an - ti - co
fold - ing sea - son; yet she lets an - cient
gion no - vel - la ser - bi l'an -
fold - ing sea - son; yet she lets

ser - bi l'an - ti - co
yet she lets an - cient

ser - bi l'an - ti - co ver - no, ser - bi l'an -
yet she lets an - cient win - ter, yet she lets

ver - - no,
win - - ter,

ti - co ver - no,
an - cient win - ter,

ser - bi l'an - ti - co ver -
yet she lets an - cient win -

ver - no, ser - bi l'an - ti - co
win - ter, yet she lets an - cient

ti - co ver - no,
an - cient win - ter,

ser - bi l'an - ti -
yet she lets -

ser - bi l'an - ti - co
yet she lets an - cient

no, ser - bi l'an - ti - co ver - no,
ter, yet she lets an - cient win - ter,
ver - no,
win - ter,
ser - bi l'an - ti - co ver - no,
yet she lets an - cient win - ter,
- co ver - no,
- cient win - ter,
ver - no,
win - ter,
deh
ah!
deh
ah!
deh s'hai pur cin - to il cor
ah! place a - bout her heart
deh s'hai pur cin - to il cor
ah! place a - bout her heart
deh s'hai pur cin - to il
ah! place a - bout her
deh
ah!
deh,
ah!

s'hai pur cin - to il cor, deh,
place a - bout her heart ah!

deh,
ah!
s'hai pur cin - to il
place a - bout her

cor,
heart,
s'hai pur cin - to il cor,
place a - bout her heart,

s'hai pur cin - to il cor,
place a - bout her heart,
s'hai pur cin - to il
place a - bout her

s'hai pur cin - to il cor
place a - bout her heart
di
e -

di
e -
ghiac - cio e
ter - nal

cor
heart
di ghiac -
e ter -

s'hai pur cin - to il cor
place a - bout her heart
di ghiac -
e - ter -

cor
heart
di ghiac -
e - ter -

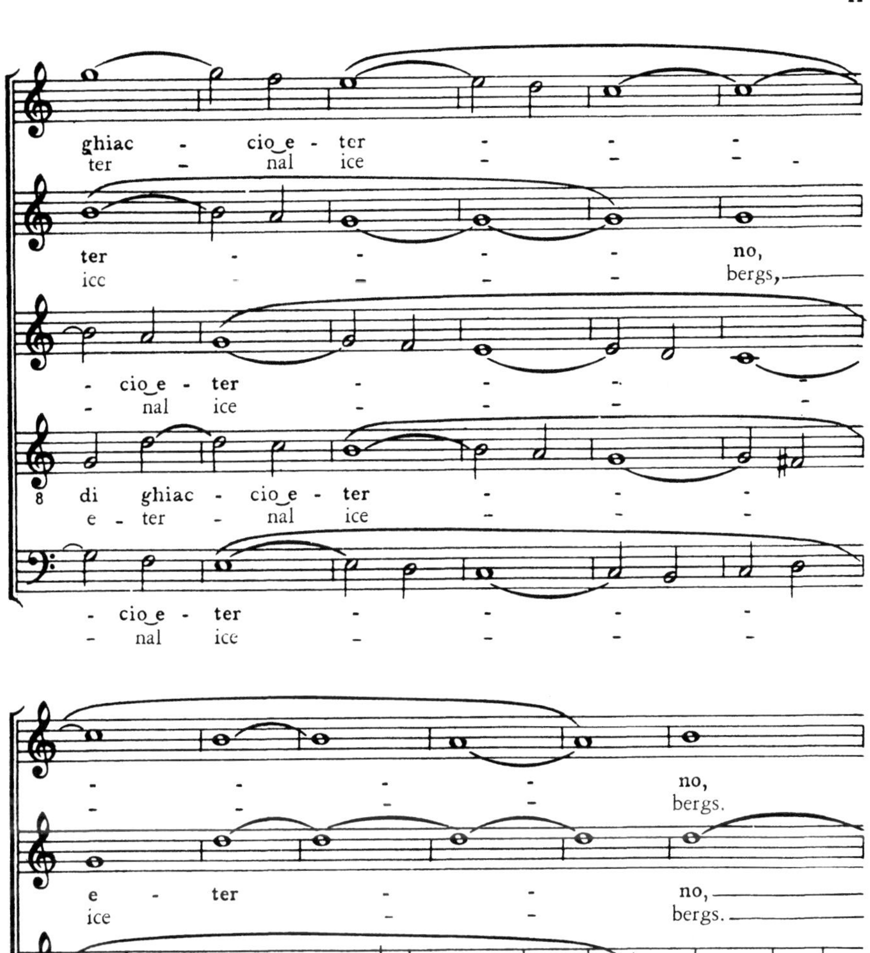

ghiac - cio_e - ter - - -
ter - nal ice - - -

ter - - - no,
icc - - - bergs,

- cio_e - ter - - -
- nal ice - - -

di ghiac - cio_e - ter - - -
e - ter - nal ice - - -

- cio_e - ter - - -
- nal ice - - -

- - - no,
- bergs.

e - ter - - no,
ice - - bergs.

no, per - chè
bergs. Why so

- - - - no,
bergs.

- - - - no,
bergs.

per - chè nin - - fa cru - del
Why so cru - - el and cold,
per - chè nin - fa cru -
Why so cru - el and
nin - - fa cru - del, per - chè nin - fa cru -
cru - - el and cold, Why so cru - el and
per - chè nin - fa cru - del
Why so cru - el and cold,
per - chè nin - - fa cru - del
Why so cru - - el and cold,

quan - to gen - ti - le, quan - to gen - ti - le, quan - to gen -
fair - est of flow - ers fair - est of flow - ers fair - est of
del quan - to gen - ti - le, quan - to gen - ti - le, quan - to gen -
cold, fair - est of flow - ers fair - est of flow - ers fair - est of
del quan - to gen - ti - le, quan - to gen -
cold, fair - est of flow - ers fair - est of
quan - to gen - ti - le, quan - to gen - ti - le,
fair - est of flow - ers fair - est of flow - ers?
quan - to gen - ti - le, quan - to gen -
fair - est of flow - ers fair - est of

ti - le
flow - ers?
ti - le
flow - ers?
por - ti ne-gl'oc-chi il sol,
Show me the smil-ing sun,
ti - le
flow - ers?
por - ti ne-gl'oc-chi il sol, nel
Show me the smil-ing sun, not
por - ti ne-gl'oc-chi il sol, nel volt'
Show me the smil-ing sun, not A -
ti - le por - ti ne-gl'oc-chi il sol, nel
flow - ers? Show me the smil-ing sun, not
por - ti ne-gl'oc-chi il sol, nel volt'
Show me the smil-ing sun, not A -
nel volt' a - pri - le, nel volt' a -
not A - pril show - ers, not A - pril
volt' a - pri - le, nel volt' a -
A - pril show - ers, not A - pril
a - pri - le,
pril show - ers!
volt' a - pri - le,
A - pril show - ers!

a - pri - le, por - ti ne-gl'oc-chi il sol,
- pril show - ers! Show me the smil-ing sun,
pri - le,
show - ers!
pri - le, por - ti ne-gl'oc-chi il sol, nel vol -
show - ers! Show me the smil-ing sun, not A -
por - ti ne-gl'oc-chi il sol, nel volt' a -
Show me the smil-ing sun, not A - pril
por - ti ne-gl'oc-chi il sol, nel volt' a -
Show me the smil-ing sun, not A - pril

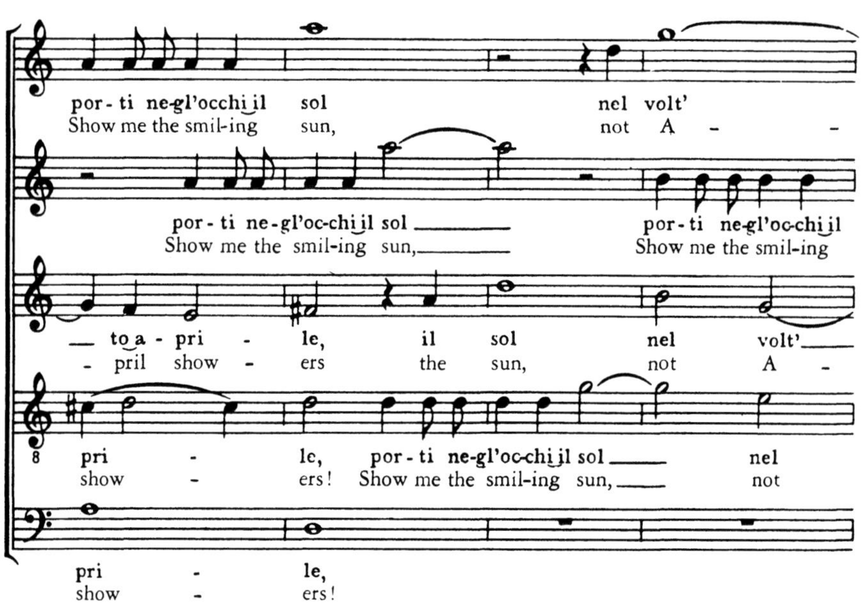
por - ti ne-gl'occhi il sol nel volt'
Show me the smil-ing sun, not A -
por - ti ne-gl'oc-chi il sol por - ti ne-gl'oc-chi il
Show me the smil-ing sun, Show me the smil-ing
to a - pri - le, il sol nel volt'
- pril show - ers the sun, not A -
pri - le, por - ti ne-gl'oc-chi il sol nel
show - ers! Show me the smil-ing sun, not
pri - le,
show - ers!

a - pri - le, nel vol -
pril show - ers, not A -
sol, nel vol - to a - pri - le, nel vol - to a - pri -
sun, not A - pril show - ers, not A - pril show -
a - pri - le, nel vol - to,
pril show - ers, not A pril
volt' a - pri - le, por - ti ne-gl'oc-chi il sol,
A - pril show - ers! Show me the smil-ing sun,
por - ti ne-gl'oc-chi il sol, nel vol -
Show me the smil-ing sun, not A -
to a - pri - le.
pril show - ers!
le.
ers!
le.
ers!
nel vol - to a - pri - le.
not A - pril show - ers!
nel vol - to a - pri - le.
not A - pril show - ers!
to a - pri - le.
pril show - ers!

# In un boschetto
## Beneath a Laurel's Branches

Luca Marenzio
ca.1560-1599

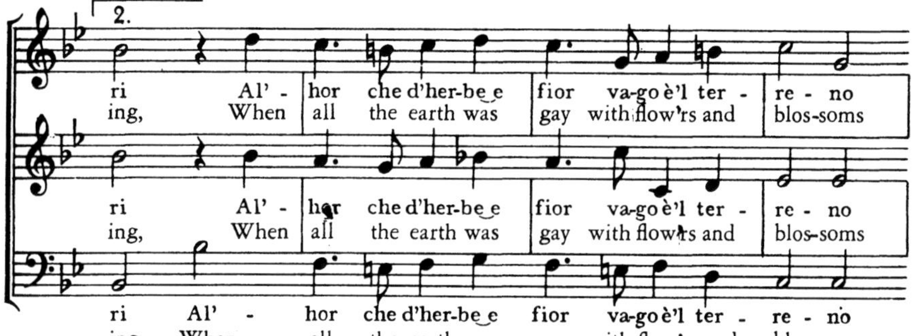

2. Dicea la Ninfa con gràte parole,
Dite caro mio ben, dolce sole,
Dov'è l'anima tua, dov'è il tuo cuore?

3. Disse al'hor il pastor con un sospiro
Pien di dolcezza, con affanno mista,
Tu sei l'anima mia, mio cuore e vita.

4. Al'hor la vaga Ninfa con un riso,
Con vezzose parole, e dolci ciancie
La bocca gli bascio, gli occhi e le guancie.

2. I heard the nymph demand with gentle teasing:
"Tell me, my dearest darling, let me hear it:
Where are your heart and soul? Who rules your spirit?

3. Then spoke the shepherd, pale with tender passion
And sighed and smiled in happy lovers' fashion:
"You are my soul, you are my heart and being."

4. Then laughed the pretty little nymph with pleasure
And called him her beloved and her treasure
And gave him kisses none shall count or measure.

Ite caldi sospiri al freddo core  
Go Forth, My Sighs

Johannes Brochus  
Venice 1504

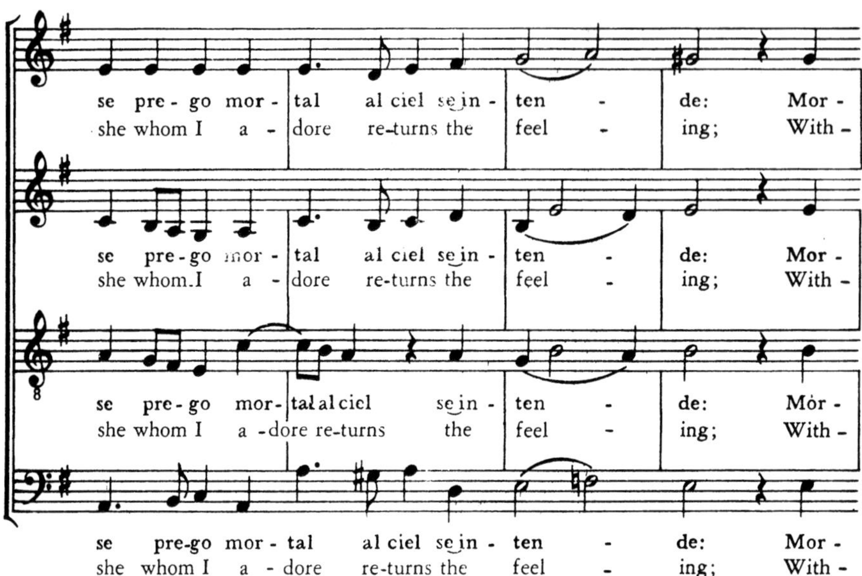
se pre - go mor - tal al ciel se in - ten - de: Mor -
she whom I a - dore re-turns the feel - ing; With -
se pre-go mor - tal al ciel se in - ten - de: Mor -
she whom I a - dore re-turns the feel - ing; With -
se pre - go mor - tal al ciel se in - ten - de: Mor -
she whom I a - dore re-turns the feel - ing; With -
se pre-go mor - tal al ciel se in - ten - de: Mor -
she whom I a - dore re-turns the feel - ing; With -

te o mer - cè, sia fi-ne al mio do - lo - re, Mor -
out her love I'll have to die of sor - row, With -
te o mer - cè, sia fi-ne al mio do - lo - re, Mor -
out her love I'll have to die of sor - row, With -
te o mer - cè, sia fi-ne al mio do - lo - re, Mor -
out her love I'll have to die of sor - row, With -
te o mer - cè, sia fi - ne al mio do - lo - re, Mor -
out her love I'll have to die of sor - row, With -

te o mer - cè, sia fi-ne al mio do - lo - re, Mor-
out her love I'll have to die of sor - row, With -

te o mer - cè, sia fi-ne al mio do - lo - re, Mor-te o mer -
out her love I'll have to die of sor - row, With- out her

te o mer - cè, sia fi-ne al mio do - lo - re, Mor-te o mer -
out her love I'll have to die of sor - row, With-out her

te o mer - cè, sia fi-ne al mio do - lo - re, Mor-te o mer -
out her love I'll have to die of sor - row, With-out her

te o mer - cè, sia fi - ne al mio do - lo - re.
out her love I'll have to die of sor - row.

cè, mer - cè, sia fi - ne al mio do - lo - re.
love, her love I'll have to die of sor - row.

cè, sia fi - ne al mio do - lo - re.
love I'll have to die of sor - row.

cè, mer - cè, sia fi - ne al mio do - lo - re.
love, her love I'll have to die of sor - row.

# El grillo
# The Cricket

Josquin Desprez
ca. 1450-1521

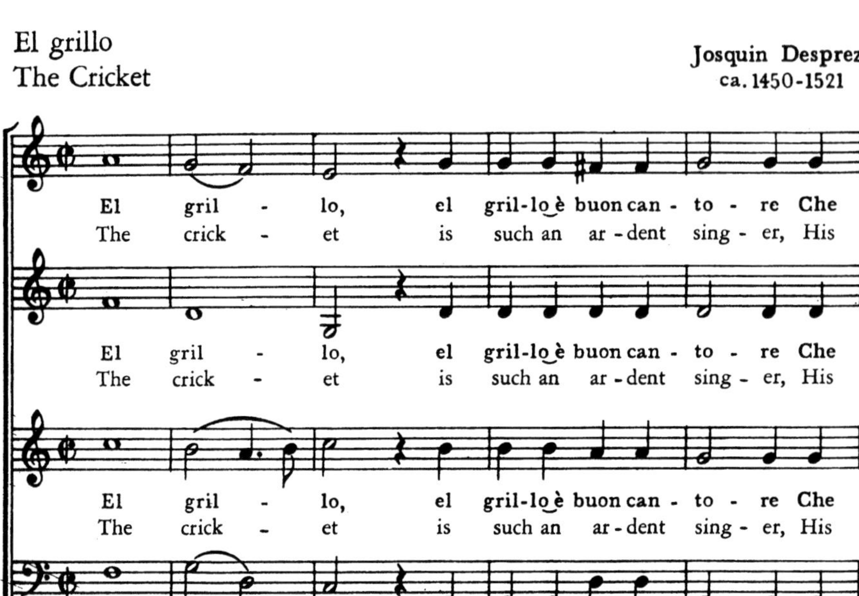


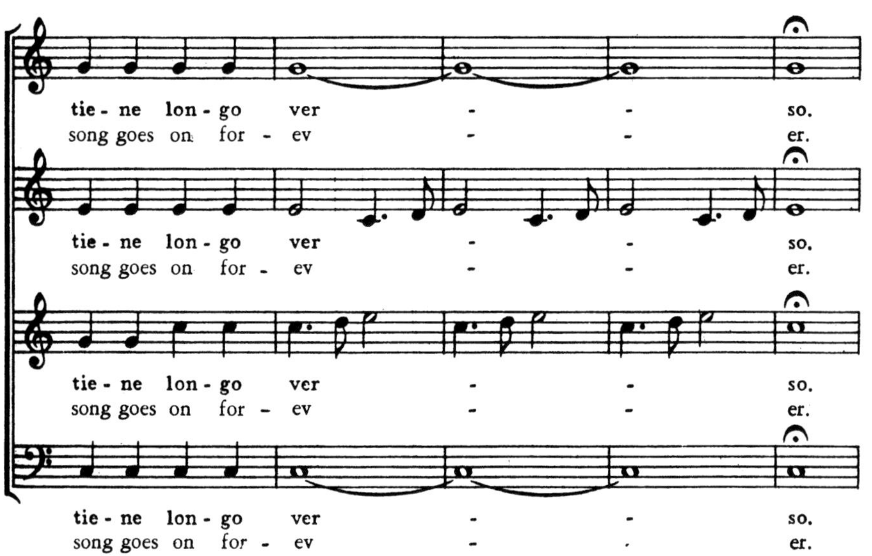

Dal - le be - ve gril - lo can - ta
Sing-ing in the dew-y mead-ow.

Dal - le be - ve gril - lo can - ta
Sing-ing in the dew-y mead-ow.

Dal - le be - ve gril - lo can - ta
Sing-ing in the dew-y mead-ow.

Dal - le be - ve gril - lo can - ta
Sing-ing in the dew-y mead-ow.

dal - le dal - le be - ve be - ve gril - lo gril - lo can - ta. El
Sing-ing, sing-ing, sing-ing in the dew-y, dew-y mead - ow; The

dal - le dal - le be - ve be - ve gril - lo gril - lo can - ta. El
Sing-ing, sing-ing, sing-ing in the dew-y, dew-y mead - ow; The

dal - le dal - le be - ve be - ve gril - lo gril - lo can - ta. El
Sing-ing, sing-ing, sing-ing in the dew-y, dew-y mead - ow; The

dal - le dal - le be - ve be - ve gril - lo gril - lo can - ta. El
Sing-ing, sing-ing, sing-ing in the dew-y, dew-y mead - ow; The

gril - lo, el gril - lo è buon can - to - re.
crick - et is such an ar - dent sing - er;

gril - lo, el gril - lo è buon can - to - re.
crick - et is such an ar - dent sing - er;

gril - lo, el gril - lo è buon can - to - re.
crick - et is such an ar - dent sing - er;

gril - lo, el gril - lo è buon can - to - re.
crick - et is such an ar - dent sing - er;

Ma non fa co - me gli al-tri uc - cel - li, Co - me
Nev - er acts like so man - y oth - ers Who will
Ma non fa co - me gli al-tri uc - cel - li, Co - me
Nev - er acts like so man - y oth - ers Who will
Ma non fa co - me gli al-tri uc - cel - li, Co - me
Nev - er acts like so man - y oth - ers Who will
Ma non fa co - me gli al-tri uc - cel - li, Co - me
Nev - er acts like so man - y oth - ers Who will
li han can - ta - to un po - co, Van' de fat -
sing a few lilt - ing mea - sures And then seek
li han can - ta - to un po - co, Van' de fat -
sing a few lilt - ing mea - sures And then seek
li han can - ta - to un po - co, Van' de fat -
sing a few lilt - ing mea - sures And then seek
li han can - ta - to un po - co, Van' de fat -
sing a few lilt - ing mea - sures And then seek
to in al - tro lo - co sem - pre el gril - lo sta pur
out more tempt - ing plea - sures. No, the brave crick-et keeps on
to in al - tro lo - co sem - pre el gril - lo sta pur
out more tempt - ing plea - sures. No, the brave crick-et keeps on
to in al - tro lo - co sem - pre el gril - lo sta pur
out more tempt - ing plea - sures. No, the brave crick-et keeps on
to in al - tro lo - co sem - pre el gril - lo sta pur
out more tempt - ing plea - sures. No, the brave crick-et keeps on

sal - do, Quan - do la mag - gior è'l
sing - ing Though the sun be hot and

sal - do, Quan - do la mag - gior è'l
sing - ing Though the sun be hot and

sal - do, Quan - do la mag - gior è'l
sing - ing Though the sun be hot and

sal - do, Quan - do la mag - gior è'l
sing - ing Though the sun be hot and

cal - do Al' hor can - ta sol per
sting - ing — Be - cause he al - ways sings

cal - do Al' hor can - ta sol per
sting - ing — Be - cause he al - ways sings

cal - do Al' hor can - ta sol per
sting - ing — Be - cause he al - ways sings

cal - do Al' hor can - ta sol per
sting - ing — Be - cause he al - ways sings

a - mo - - - re.
great love- - - - songs!

a - mo - - re.
great love- - - songs!

a - mo - - - re.
great love- - - - songs!

a - mo - - re.
great love- - songs!

# Vorria che tu cantass una canzon
## A Sweet New Song

Antonio Scandello
1517-1580

e che di-ces - si, e che di-ces - si: fa mi la mi sol
And you'd be say - ing, And you'd be say - ing:
che di-ces - si, e che di-ces - si: fa mi
you'd be say - ing, And you'd be say - ing:
ces - si e che di-ces - si: fa mi la mi sol la mi sol
say - ing, And you'd be say - ing:
che di-ces - si e che di-ces - si: fa mi la mi sol
you'd be say - ing, And you'd be say - ing:

la fa mi fa mi la mi sol la fa mi la mi sol la fa mi la mi
la mi sol la fa mi la mi sol la mi sol la la mi sol la fa
la fa mi la mi sol la fa mi la mi sol la fa mi la mi
la fa mi la mi sol la fa mi la mi sol la mi sol la fa mi la mi

1.
sol la fa mi la mi sol la.
mi la mi sol la fa mi la mi sol la. E
And
sol la fa mi la mi sol la. E che di-
And you'd be
sol la fa mi la mi sol la. E
And

2.
la.
la.
la.
la.

## Allons, gai bergères
## Come, Ye Shepherds

Guillaume Costeley
1531-1606

ciel en ter - re est né. Gai, gai. Al - lons, gai, gai, gai ber - gè - res,
down to earth for us. Oh joy! Come, ye shep-herds, strong and a - ble,
ter - re et né. Gai, gai gai, gai. Al - lons, gai, gai, gai ber - gè - res,
earth for us. Oh joy! Oh joy! Come, ye shep-herds, strong and a - ble,
ciel en ter-re est né. Gai, gai. Al - lons, gai, gai, gai ber - gè - res,
down to earth for us. Oh joy! Come, ye shep-herds, strong and a - ble,
Al - lons, gai, gai, gai ber - gè - res,
Come, ye shep-herds, strong and a - ble,

al - lons, gai, al - lons, gai, soy - ez lé - gè - res, sui-vez moi.
Come a -long! Let us go and find the sta - ble. Fol-low me!
al - lons, gai, al - lons, gai, soy - ez lé - gè - res, sui-vez moi.
Come a -long! Let us go and find the sta - ble. Fol-low me!
al - lons, gai, al - lons, gai, soy - ez lé - gè - res, sui - vez moi. Un beau
Come a -long! Let us go and find the sta-ble. Fol - low me! Say, what
al - lons, gai, al - lons, gai, soy - ez lé - gè - res, sui - vez moi.
Come a -long! Let us go and find the sta - ble. Fol-low me!

Un beau pré - sent lui fe - rai. De ce fla - geol -
Say, what pres-ent shall I bring? I'll bring him this
Un beau pré - sent lui fe - rai, de quoi? De ce
Say, what pres - ent shall I bring the King? I'll bring
pré sent lui fe - rai, de quoi? De ce fla-geol-
pres-ent shall I bring the King? I'll bring him this
de quoi?
the King?

let, que j'ai,que j'ai tant gai. Al - lons,gai,gai,gai,ber - gè -res, al -lons,
flute so gay, so gay to play. Come, ye shep-herds,quick and a -ble, come a -
flageollet,que j'ai,que j'ai tant gai. Al -lons,gai,gai, gai,ber - gè-res, al -lons,
him this flute so gay, so gay to play. Come,ye shep-herds,quick and a - ble, come a -
let,que j'ai,que j'ai tant gai. Al -lons,gai,gai, gai,ber - gè-res, al -lons,
flute so gay, so gay to play. Come,ye shep-herds,quick and a -ble, come a -
Al -lons,gai,gai,gai,ber - gè-res, al -lons,
Come,ye shep-herds,quick and a - ble, come a -
gai, al - lons,gai,soy- ez lé - gè - res, sui -vez moi. Un gâ-teau lui
long! Let us find that bless-ed sta - ble, fol -low me! Here's a cake I'll
gai, al - lons,gai,soy- ez lé - gè - res, sui -vez moi. Un gâ-
long! Let us find that bless-ed sta - ble, fol -low me! Here's a
gai, al -lons, gai,soy- ez lé - gè-res,sui - vez moi.
long! Let us find that bless-ed sta-ble, fol - low me!
gai, al - lons, gai,soy- ez lé - gè - res, sui -vez. moi.
long! Let us find that bless-ed sta - ble, fol-low me!
don - ne - rai, un gâ- teau lui don - ne - rai.
take and bring. Here's a cake I'll take and bring.
teau lui don-ne-rai lui don - ne -rai. Et moi?
cake I'll take and bring, this I will bring. And here
Un gâ-teau lui don - ne - rai. Et moi?
Here's a cake I'll take and bring. And here
Et moi?Plein ha-
And here plums and

gai,gai. Al - lons,gai,gai. gai,ber-gè - res,
Oh joy! Come, ye shep-herds,swift and a - ble,
Plein hanap lui of-fri - rai, gai, gai. Al - lons,gai,gai, gai,ber-gè-res,al-
plums and ap - ples for the King. Oh joy! Come, ye shep-herds,swift and a-ble,come -
Plein hanap lui of-fri - rai, gai, gai. Al - lons gai, gai, gai, ber-gè - res,
plums and ap - ples for the King. Oh joy! Come, ye shep - herds, swift and a - ble,
nap lui of - fri - rai, gai, gai. Al - lons gai,gai, gai,ber-gè - res,
ap - ples for the King. Oh joy! Come, ye shep-herds,swift and a - ble,
al - lons, gai, al - lons,gai,soy - ez lé - gè - res, sui-vez-moi.
come with me, Let us go and find the sta - ble. Fol-low me!
- lons,gai, al - lons,gai, soy - ez le - gè-res, sui - vez - moi.
with me, Let us go and find the sta-ble. Fol - low me!
al-lons, gai, al - lons,gai,soy - ez lé - gè - res, sui-vez-moi
come with me, Let us go and find the sta - ble. Fol-low me!
al-lons, gai, al - lons,gai, soy - ez lé - gè - res, sui-vez-moi Ho
come with me, Let us go and find the sta - ble. Fol-low me! Ho
Ho, ho, Paix-la, paix - la, je le vois;
Ho ho! Look there! He's there! Full of zest
Ho, ho, paix paix - la je le vois,je le vois;Il tê-
Ho ho! Look He's there!Full of zest,Full of zest.Nursing
Ho, ho,Paix - la paix - la je le vois,je le vois;
Ho ho! Look He's there! And full of zest,Full of zest
ho; Paix, - la paix paix-la je le vois,je le vois;
ho! Look He's there! He's there!Full of zest,Full of zest

il tet- te bien sans le doigt, il tet- te bien sans le doigt,le pe-tit
Nurs-ing at his Moth-er's breast, Nurs-ing at his Moth-er's breast,the lit-tle
te bien, il tet- te bien sans le doigt,sans le doigt,le pe-tit
Yes,He's nurs ing at Moth er's breast, at Moth-er's breast,the lit-tle
il tet- te bien sans le doigt, il tet- te bien sans le doigt, ___
Nurs-ing at his Moth-er's breast, Nurs-ing at his Moth-er's breast, ___
il tet - te bien sans le doigt, ___
Nurs-ing at his Moth - er's breast, ___
roi gai, gai. Al - lons, gai,gai,gai,ber - gè-res, al lons, gai, al lons,
King. Oh joy! Come, ye shep-herds,glad and a -ble, Come a - long! Come,I'll
roi gai, gai. Al - lons, gai,gai,gai,ber - gè-res, al -lons, gai, al -lons,
King. Oh joy! Come, ye shep-herds,glad and a -ble, Come a - long! Come,I'll
___ le pe-tit roi. Al - lons, gai,gai, gai, ber - gè-res, al - lons, gai, al-lons,
___ the lit-tle King.Come, ye shep-herds, glad and a -ble, Come a - long!Come,I'll
___ le pe-tit roi. Al - lons, gai, gai, gai, ber - gè-res, al-lons, gai, al-lons,
___ the lit-tle King.Come, ye shep-herds,glad and a -ble, Come a - long! Come,I'll
gai, soy-ez lé - gè - res, le roi boit, le roi boit.
take you to the sta - ble. See the King! See him rest!
gai, soy-ez lé - gè-res, le roi boit,le roi boit. ___
take you to the sta-ble. See the King!See him rest! ___
gai, soy-ez lé - gè-res, le roi boit, le roi boit.
take you to the __ sta-ble. See the King! See him rest!
gai, soy-ez lé - gè - res, le roi boit, le roi boit.
take you to the sta - ble. See the King! See him rest!

# Belle qui tiens ma vie
## Fair Maiden, You Have Captured

Toinot Arbeau
16th Century

## Filles à marier
## Better Do Not Get Married

Gilles Binchois
ca. 1400-1467

jà, ne vous ma - ri - ez jà, ne vous ma - ri - ez jà,
maid, you pret-ty lit - tle maid, you pret-ty lit - tle maid!
ne vous ma - ri - ez jà, ne vous ma - ri - ez jà,
you pret-ty lit - tle maid, you pret-ty lit - tle maid!
ri - ez jà.
ry, sweet maid!
ma - ri - ez jà.
mar - ry, sweet maid!
Car se ja - lou - sie a, ja - lou - sie
If he's a jeal - ous man a jeal - ous
Car se ja - lou - sie a,
If he's a jeal - ous man,
Car se ja - lou - sie a,
If he's a jeal - ous man,
Car se ja -
If he's jeal -
a ja - mais ne vous ne lui, ja
man Too soon for him and you Love's
ja - lou-sie a ja - mais ne vous ne lui, ja-mais ne vous ne
a jeal-ous man Too soon for him and you Love's joy is bound to
Car se ja - lou - sie
If he's jeal - ous of
lou - sie a, ja - lou - sie
ous of you, jeal - ous - of

mais, ja-mais ne vous ne lui au cuer joy-e n'a-
joy, Love's joy is bound to fade. Love's joy is bound to
lui au cuer joy-e n'a-ra
fade, Love's joy is bound to fade.
a au cuer
you Love's joy
a au
you Love's
ra joy-e n'a-ra au
fade. is bound to fade, Love's
au cuer joy-e n'a-ra joy-e n'a-ra
Love's joy is bound to fade, is bound to fade,
joy - e n'a - ra
is bound to fade.
cuer joy - e au
joy, love's joy love's
cuer joy - e n'a - ra.
joy will fade, will fade.
au cuer joy-e n'a-ra, au cuer joy-e n'a-ra.
Love's joy is bound to fade, Love's joy is bound to fade.
au cuer joy - e n'a - ra.
Love's joy is bound to fade.
cuer joy - e n'a - ra.
joy is bound to fade.

# Je suis déshéritée
## Oh, I Have Been Forsaken

Jacob (Jacotin) Godebrye
† 1529

m'a lais - sé - e,
pale and shak - en,
plei - ne de
To weep, to
- e,
- en,
plei - ne de
To weep, to
pleurs et de sou - ci, de
wor - ry and to grieve, weep
e,
en,
plei - ne de pleurs et de sou - ci, et
To weep, to wor - ry and to grieve, to

pleurs et de sou - ci.
wor - ry and to grieve.
Ros - sig -
Pret - ty
sou - ci.
and grieve.
Ros - sig - nol du
Pret - ty night-in - gale a -
bois jo -
de sou - ci.
weep and grieve.
Ros - sig - nol du bois
Pret - ty night-in - gale

nol du bois jo -
night-in - gale a -
li, sans point
bove, Fly a - way with-out de
fai - re de - meu
li,
bove,
sans point fai - re
Fly a - way with - out de
de - meu
jo - li,
a - bove,
sans point fai - re de - meu
Fly a - way with-out de

re,
lay
va - t'en di - re à mon a -
And when at last you find my
- re, va - t'en di - re à mon a - mi, à mon
- lay And when at last you find my love, you find
re, va - t'en di - re à mon a - mi, à mon
lay And when at last you find my love, you find
mi, que pour lui suis tourmen - té -
love Tell him that my heart is ail -
- a - mi, que pour lui suis tour-men - té
- my love Tell him that my heart is ail -
- a - mi, que pour lui suis tour - men - té -
- my love Tell him that my heart is ail -
e, que pour lui suis tour-men - té - e.
ing. Tell him that my heart is ail - ing.
e, que pour lui suis tour-men - té - e.
ing. Tell him that my heart is ail - ing.
e, que pour lui suis tour - men - té - e.
ing. Tell him that my heart is ail - ing.

# Tourdion (Quand je bois du vin clairet)
## When I'm Drinking Good Red Wine

Anonym
16th Century

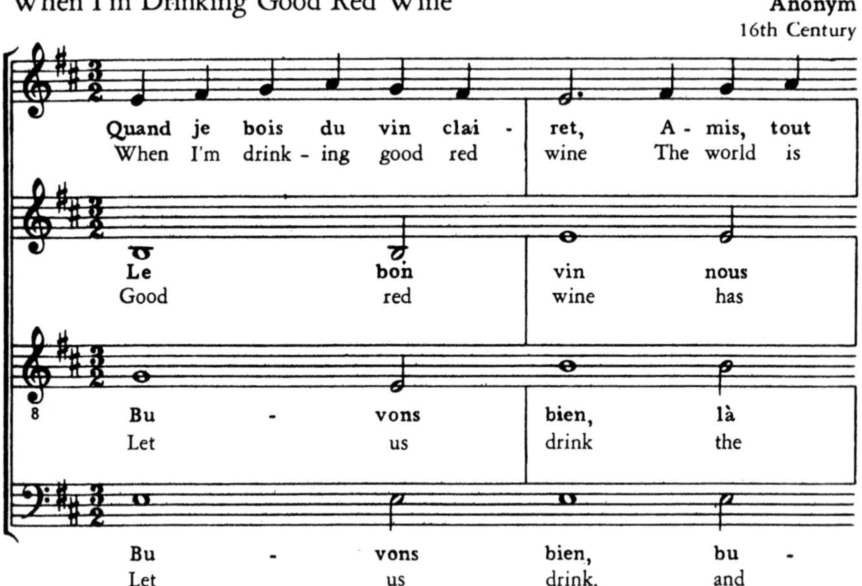

FINE
bois An - jou ou Ar - bois.
gay When I drink Ar - ro - sé.
Chan-tons et bu -
Sing - ing, we will

ou-bli-ons nos pei - nes, chan - tons.
what has made us sad; Drink and sing!
En man - us
Let us

con fai - sons la guerre.
bot - tle last too long!
En man -
Let us

vons, vi - dons nos verres.
wine will make you strong.
En man -
Let us

vons, à ce fla - con fai - sons la guer - re,
drink and cheer-ful - ly fin - ish the bot - tle.

geant d'un gras jam - bon, à
eat a juic - y roast And

geant d'un gras jam - bon, à
eat a juic - y roast And

geant d'un gras jam - bon, à
eat a juic - y roast And

D.C.
chan - tons et bu - vons, mes a - mis, bu - vons donc.
Come, let us be hap - py, my friends. Drink and sing!

ce fla - con fai - sons la guerre.
drink a toast And sing a song!

ce fla - con fai - sons la guerre.
drink a toast And sing a song!

ce fla - con fai - sons la guerre.
drink a toast And sing a song!

# Francion vint l'autre jour
## Gabriel, The Other Day

Pierre Bonnet
16th Century

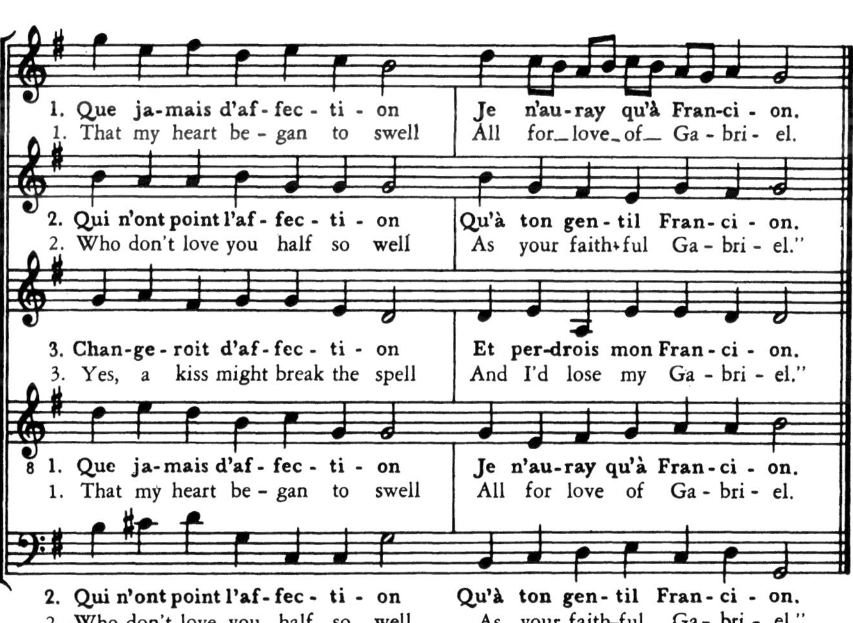


2. Qui n'ont point l'af - fec - ti - on Qu'à ton gen - til Fran-ci - on.
2. Who don't love you half so well As your faith-ful Ga - bri - el."

Mas vale trocar
Far Better to Feel

Juan Encina
1469-ca.1530

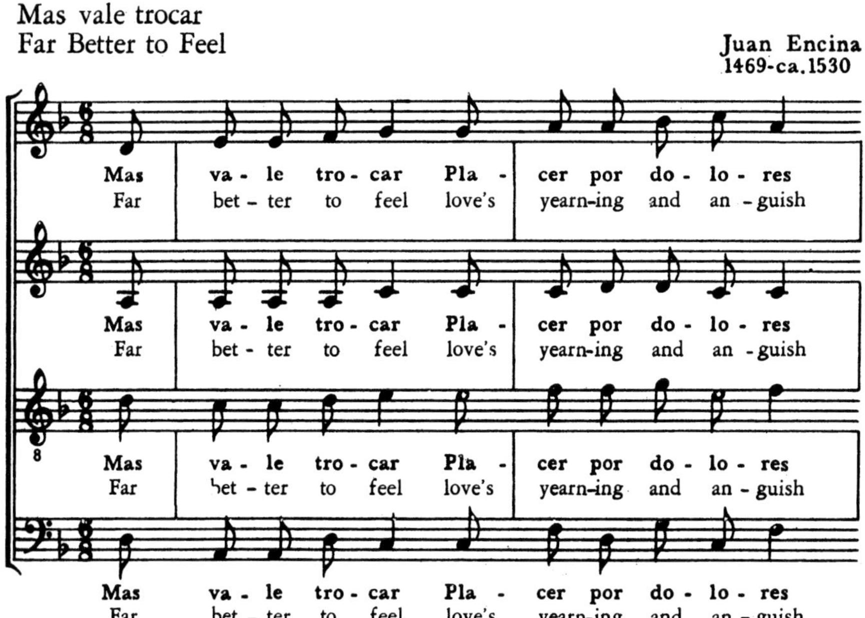


FINE

Don - de es gra - de - ci - do Es dul - ce mo - rir Vi -
Where you are, be - lov - ed, There I would be, too; For,

Don - de es gra - de - ci - do Es dul - ce mo - rir Vi -
Where you are, be - lov - ed, There I would be, too; For,

Don - de es gra - de - ci - do Es dul - ce mo - rir Vi -
Where you are, be - lov - ed, There I would be, too; For,

Don - de es gra - de - ci - do Es dul - ce mo - rir Vi -
Where you are, be - lov - ed, There I would be, too; For,


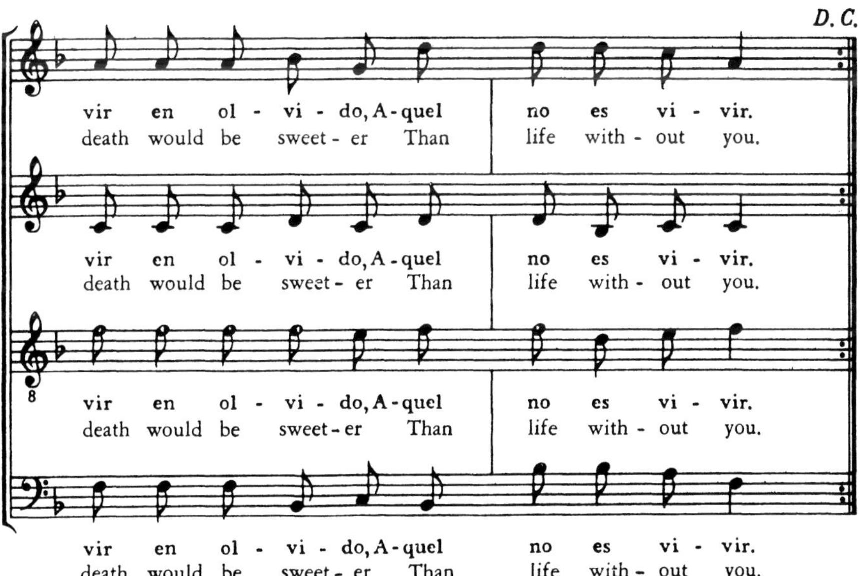

D. C.

vir en ol - vi - do, A - quel no es vi - vir.
death would be sweet - er Than life with - out you.

vir en ol - vi - do, A - quel no es vi - vir.
death would be sweet - er Than life with - out you.

vir en ol - vi - do, A - quel no es vi - vir.
death would be sweet - er Than life with - out you.

vir en ol - vi - do, A - quel no es vi - vir.
death would be sweet - er Than life with - out you.

# Congoxa mas
## Oh, My Heart Is Sad and Sore

Juan Encina
1469-ca.1530

sin me___ par - tir. De vos, gra - cio - say___
one I___ a - dore Dark is the sky, dark___
sin me par - tir. De vos, gra - cio -
one I a - dore Dark is the sky,___
sin me___ par - tir. De vos, gra - cio - say___
one I ___ a - dore Dark is the sky, dark___
___ sen - ti - da. Con - go - xa___ mas que
each_ long day. Oh, my heart___ is sad___
say sen - ti - da. Con - go - xa___ mas que
dark each long day. Oh, my heart is sad
___ sen - ti - da. Con - go - xa mas
each_long day. Oh, my heart is
___ cru - el Com-ba - te mi tri - ste
___ and sore. Hope and joy have both___ de -
___ cru - el Com-ba - te___ mi___ tri - ste
___ and sore. Hope and joy___ have___ both_de -
que___ cru - el Com-ba - te mi___ tri - ste
sad ___ and sore. Hope and joy have___ both_de -
vi - da. La cau - sa fué mi par - ti - da.
part - ed. Cru - el fate, you call me___ a - way.
vi - da. La cau - sa fué___ mi___ par - ti - da.
part - ed. Cru - el fate,_you___ call___ me_a - way.
vi - da. La cau - sa fué mi par - ti - da.
part - ed. Cru - el_ fate, you call me___ a - way.

# Ah, the sighs that come from my heart

Robert Cornysh
1465-1523

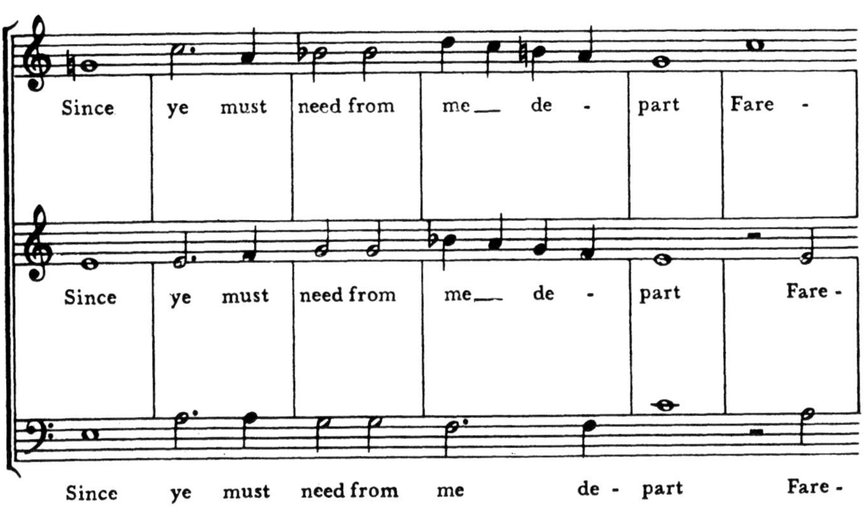

Since ye must need from me de - part Fare -
Since ye must need from me de - part Fare -
Since ye must need from me de - part Fare -

well my joy for e - ver - more.
well my joy for e - ver - more.
well my joy for e - - ver - more.

# Hard by a fountain

Hubert Waelrant
1518-1595

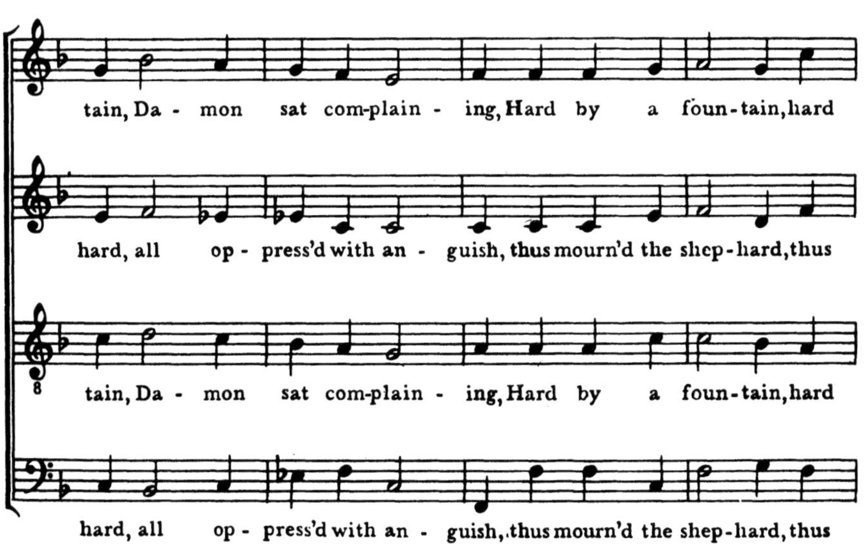

by a foun - tain, Da - mon sat com-plain - ing. Of
mourn'd the shep - hard, all op - press'd with an - guish. O
by a foun - tain, Da - mon sat com-plain - ing. Of
mourn'd the shep - hard, all op - press'd with an - guish. O
Daph - ne fair and her un - kind dis - dain - ing, And
cru - el maid, for ev - er must I lan - guish? Fa
Daph - ne fair and her un - kind dis - dain - ing,
cru - el maid, for ev - er must I lan - guish?
ev - er and a - non, and ev - er and a - non, and
la la la la la, fa la la la la la, fa
And ev - er and a - non, and ev - er and a -
Fa la la la la la, fa la la la la

ev - er and a - non, he sad - ly sigh - ed, he sad - ly
la la la la la, the nymph re - pli - ed, the nymph re -
non, he sad - ly sigh - ed, he sad - ly
la, the nymph re - pli - ed, the nymph re -
sigh - ed. And ev - er and a - non, and ev - er and a - non, and
pli - ed, fa la la la la la, fa la la la la la, fa
sigh - ed. And ev - er and a - non, and ev - er and a -
pli - ed, fa la la la la la, fa la la la la
ev - er and a - non, he sad - ly sigh - ed.
la la la la la, the nymph re pli ed.
non, he sad - ly sigh - ed.
la, the nymph re - pli - ed.

# Sing we and chant it

Thomas Morley
1557-1603

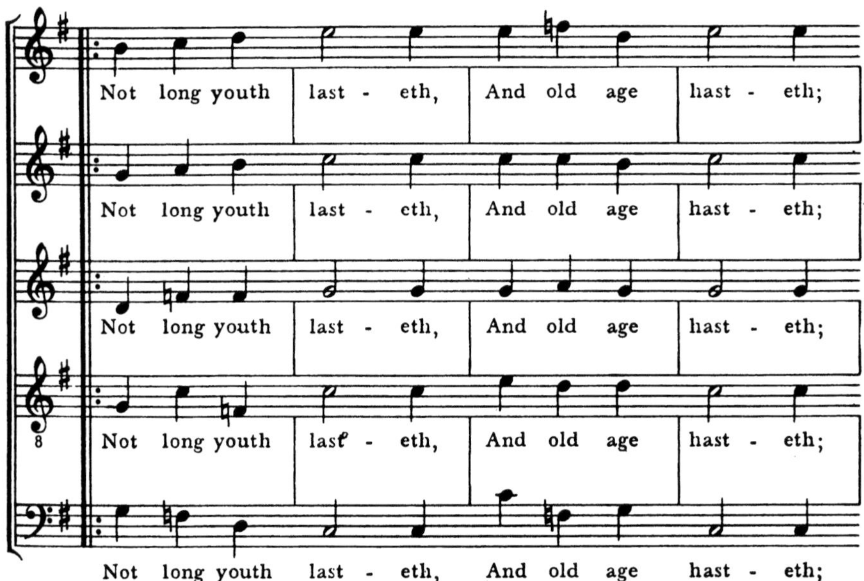
Not long youth last - eth, And old age hast - eth;
Not long youth last - eth, And old age hast - eth;
Not long youth last - eth, And old age hast - eth;
Not long youth last - eth, And old age hast - eth;
Not long youth last - eth, And old age hast - eth;

Now is best leis - ure To take our pleas - ure.
Now is best leis - ure To take our pleas - ure.
Now is best leis - ure To take our pleas - ure.
Now is best leis - ure To take our pleas - ure.
Now is best leis - ure To take our pleas - ure.

Fa la la la la
Fa la la la la la la,
Fa la la la, Fa la
Fa la la la la, Fa la
Fa la la la la la la, Fa la

la, Fa la la la la.
Fa la la la, Fa la la la.
la la la la la la, Fa la la la la.
la la la la la, Fa la la la la.
la la la la la la la.

# Grace, my lovely one, fair beauties

Thomas Weelkes
1578-1623

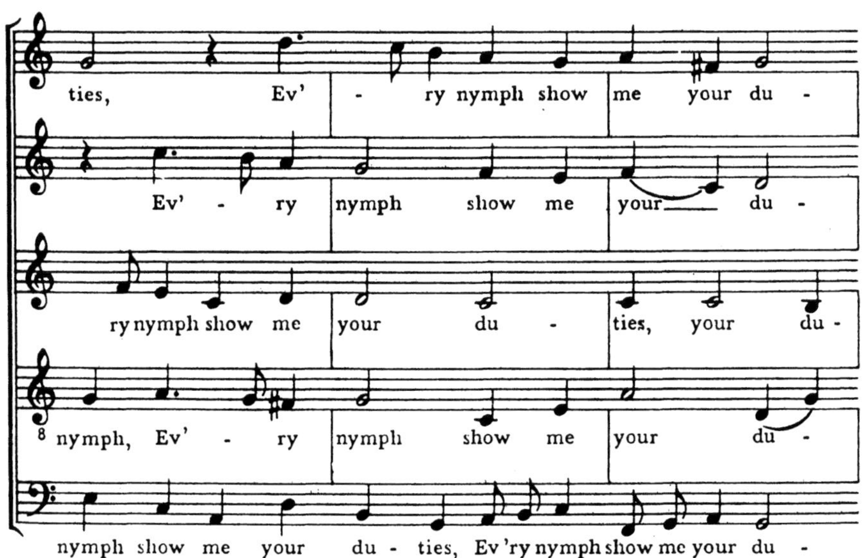

ties, Fa la la la la la la la la la la la la la
ties, Fa la la la la la la la la la la la la la la la
ties, Fa la la la la la la la la la la la la
ties, Fa la la la la la la la la la la la la la la la la la la la la la la la la

At-tend with mirth and fa - la - lays, Whilst this my love so
At-tend with mirth and fa - la lays, Whilst this my love so
At-tend with mirth and fa - la - lays, Whilst this my love so
At-tend with mirth and fa - la - lays, Whilst this my love so
At-tend with mirth and fa - la-lays, Whilst this my love so

kind - ly stays, And then I'll joy that joys of -
kind - ly stays, And then I'll joy that joys of
kind - ly stays, And then I'll joy that joys of
kind - ly stays, And then I'll joy that joys of
kind - ly stays, And then I'll joy that joys of

mine Shall thus be graced by Gra - ces nine,
mine Shall thus be graced by Gra - ces nine, Fa la
mine Shall thus be graced by Gra - ces nine, Fa la
mine Shall thus be graced by Gra - ces nine,
mine Shall thus be graced by Gra - ces nine, Fa la

Fa la la la la la la la la la la la la
la la la la la la la la la la la la la
la la la la la la la la la la la la la la la
Fa la la la la la la la la la la la la la
la la la la la la la la la la la la la la la la la la

la la la la la la la la la la.
la la la la la la la la la.
la la la la la la la la la la.
la la la la la la la la la.
la la la la la la la la la la la.

# To the hills and the vales

Henry Purcell
1658-1695

tri - umphs of love and of beau - ty be
- umphs, the tri - umphs of love and of beau - ty be
tri - umphs, the tri - umphs of love and of beau - ty be
tri - umphs of love and of beau - ty be
shown. Let the tri - umphs, let the tri -
shown. Let the tri - umphs, the tri - umphs, the
shown. Let the tri - umphs, let the tri - umphs, the
shown. Let the tri - umphs, let the tri - umphs, the tri -
umphs of love and of beau - ty be shown. To the
tri - umphs of love and of beau - ty be shown. To the
tri - umphs of love and of beau - ty be shown. To the
umphs of love and of beau - ty be shown. To the

hills and the vales, to the rocks and the moun-tains, to the
hills and the vales, to the rocks and the moun-tains, to the
hills and the vales, to the rocks and the moun-tains, to the
hills and the vales, to the rocks and the moun-tains, to the
mu - si - cal groves and the cool sha - dy foun-tains, Let the
mu - si - cal groves and the cool sha - dy foun-tains, Let the
mu - si - cal groves and the cool sha - dy foun-tains, Let the
mu - si - cal groves and the cool sha - dy foun-tains, Let the
tri - umphs, let the tri - umphs of
tri-umphs, the tri - umphs, the tri-umphs of
tri - umphs, let the tri-umphs, the tri-umphs of
tri-umphs, let the tri-umphs, the tri - umphs of

love and of beau - ty be shown. Go
love and of beau - ty be shown.
love and_ of_ beau - ty be shown. Go rev - el, ye
love and of beau - ty be shown. Go rev - el, go
rev - el, ye Cu - pids, go rev - el, go rev - el, ye
Go rev - el, ye Cu - pids, go rev - el, go
Cu - pids, go rev - el, go rev - el, ye Cu - pids, go
rev - el ye Cu - pids, go rev - el, go rev - el, ye
Cu - pids, go rev - el the day is your own.
rev - el, ye Cu - pids, the day is your_ own.
rev - el, ye Cu - pids, the day is your_ own.
Cu - pids, ye Cu - pids, the day is your own.

Oh, Nightingale
Johann Hermann Schein
1586-1630

1. Oh, night - in - gale, In grove and
2. My heart and mind No rest could
3. Ah, Lil - ly dear, It's bliss to

dale How sweet your song Rang all night long!
find. And think - ing of My Lil - ly's love
hear A bird pro - claim Your charm - ing name.

dale How sweet your song Rang all night long!
find. And think - ing of My Lil - ly's love
hear A bird pro - claim Your charm - ing name.

dale How sweet your song Rang all. night long!
find. And think - ing of My Lil .- ly's love
hear A bird pro - claim Your charm - ing name.

dale How sweet your song Rang all night long!
find. And think - ing of My Lil - ly's love
hear A bird pro - claim Your charm - ing name.

You sang my dar - ling Lil - ly's fame, You sang my dar - ling
I wan-dered through the moon - lit glade, I wan-dered through the
Much great - er still would be my bliss, Much great - er still would

You sang my dar - ling Lil - ly's fame, You sang my dar - ling
I wan-dered through the moon - lit glade I wan-dered through the
Much great- er still would be my bliss Much great- er still would

You sang my dar - ling Lil - ly's fame, You sang my dar - ling
I wan-dered through the moon - lit glade, I wan-dered through the
Much great- er still would be my bliss, Much great- er still would

Lil - ly's fame A thou-sand times
moon - lit glade And lis - tened to
be my bliss Could I but have

Lil - ly's fame A thou-sand times, a thou-sand
moon - lit glade And lis -tened to, And lis - tened
be my bliss Could I but have, Could I but

Lil - ly's fame A thou-sand times, a thou-sand
moon - lit glade And lis -. tened to, And lis -tened
be my bliss Could I but have, Could I but

a thou-sand times,
And lis -tened to,
Could I but have,
a thou-sand times,
And lis -tened to,
Could I but have,
times,
to,
have,
a thou-sand times,
And lis -tened to,
Could I but have,
a thou sand
And lis -tened
Could I but
times,
to,
have,
a thou-sand times,
And lis -tened to,
Could I but have,
a thou-sand
And lis -tened
Could I but
a thou-sand times you praised
And lis-tened to the ser -
Could I but have your lips
times, a thou-sand times you praised
to, And lis-tened to the ser -
have, Could I but have your lips
times, a thou sand times you praised her, you praised her, you
to, the ser - e - nade, ser - e - nade, ser - e - nade, ser -
have, Could I but have your sweet lips! Your sweet lips! Your
her name.
e - nade.
to kiss!
her name.
e - nade.
to kiss!
praised her, A thou-sand times you praised her name.
e - nade. And lis - tened to the ser - e - nade.
sweet lips! Could I but have your lips to kiss!

## Come, Pretty Maid

Valentin Haussmann
ca. 1600

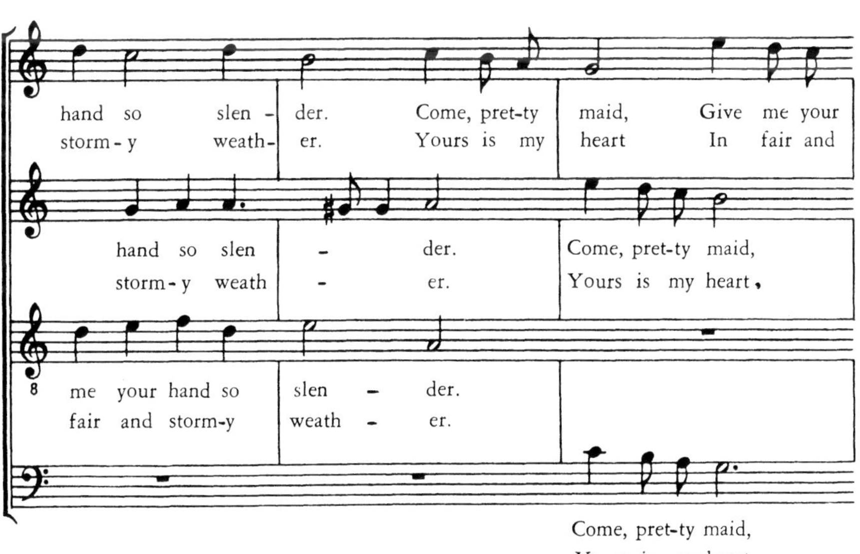

hand so slen - der.
storm- y weath- er,
Give me your
In fair and
Come, pret-ty maid, Give me
Yours is my heart In fair
your hand so
and storm - y
Come, pret-ty maid, Give
Yours is my heart In
me your
fair and
hand
storm -
Give me your
In fair and
hand so slen - der. Give me your
storm- y weath - er, In fair and
hand so slen - der.
storm y weath -
der.
er.
der.
er.
Don't be a -
No more a
slen -
weath -
der.
er.
der.
er.
Don't
No
be a - fraid:
more a part
so slen -
y weath -
der.
er.
der.
er.
Don't
No
hand so slen
storm y weath
der.
er.
der.
er.
Don't
No
be
more
a
a
fraid:
part
Don't be a -
No more a
fraid: My love is
part Let's al - ways
Don't be a -
No more a
fraid:
part
Don't
No
be a - fraid:
more a part
be a - fraid: Don't
more a part No
be a - fraid:
more a part:
My
Let's
fraid:
part
Don't be a - fraid: My
No more a part Let's
love is true and
al - ways be to -

true and ten - der. Don't
be to - geth - er! No
love is true and ten - der. Don't
al - ways be to - geth - er! No
love is true and ten der. Don't
al ways be to geth er! No
ten - - der.
geth - - er!
be a - fraid: Don't be a - fraid: My
more a part No more a part Let's
be a - fraid: Don't be a -
more a part No more a
be a - fraid: Don't be a - fraid: My love is
more, a part No more a part Let's al - ways
Don't be a - fraid: My
No more a part Let's
love is true and ten - der.
al - ways be to - geth - er!
fraid: My love is true and ten - der.
part Let's al - ways be to - geth - er!
true and ten - - der.
be to - geth - - er!
love is true and ten - - der.
al - ways be to - geth - - er!

# Ach Lieb, ich tu dir klagen
## Dear Love, You May Believe Me

Hans Leo Hassler
1564-1612

1.
2.
ich muß tra - gen, die gro-ßen Schmerzen mein, die ich muß tra - gen. gen.
come to grieve me. What bit-ter, bit - ter pain has come to grieve me. me.
ich muß tra - gen, die ich muß tra - gen. gen.
come to grieve me, has come to grieve me. me.
ich muß tra - gen, die ich muß tra - gen. gen.
come to grieve me, has come to grieve me. me.
ich muß tra - gen, die gro-ßen Schmerzen mein, die ich muß tra - gen. gen.
come to grieve me, What bit-ter, bit - ter pain has come to grieve me. me.
ich muß tra - gen, die gro-ßen Schmerzen mein, die ich muß tra - gen. gen.
come to grieve me, What bit-ter, bit - ter pain has come to grieve me. me.

O sü - ßer Trost, mein Le - ben, kehr dich zu mir, kehr dich zu
Sweet friend whose love I cher - ish, Oh, turn to me! Oh, turn to
O sü - ßer Trost, mein Le - ben, kehr dich zu mir, kehr dich zu
Sweet friend whose love I cher - ish, Oh, turn to me! Oh, turn to
O sü - ßer Trost, mein Le - ben, kehr dich zu mir,
Sweet friend whose love I cher - ish, Oh, turn to me!
O sü - ßer Trost, mein Le - ben, kehr dich zu
Sweet friend whose love I cher - ish, Oh, turn to
O sü - ßer Trost, mein Le - ben, kehr dich zu
Sweet friend whose love I cher - ish, Oh, turn to

mir, tu freund-lich mit ___ mir scher - zen, ver-kehr,
me! And let for-ev- - er af - ter My tears
mir, tu freund - lich mit mir scher - zen, ver -
me! And let ___ for-ev-er af - ter My
tu ___ freund - lich mit mir scher - zen, ver -
And ___ let for-ev-er af - ter My
mir, tu freund-lich mit ___ mir scher - zen,
me! And let for-ev - er af - ter
mir, ver -
me! My

ver-kehr in Freud mein Schmer - zen, sonst
My tears be changed to laugh - ter Or
kehr in Freud mein Schmerzen, sonst
tears be changed to laugh-ter Or
kehr, ver - kehr in Freud mein Schmer - zen, sonst
tears My tears be changed to laugh - ter Or
ver - kehr in Freud mein ___ Schmer - zen, sonst
My tears be changed to ___ laugh - ter Or
kehr, ver - kehr in Freud mein Schmer - zen,
tears My tears be changed to laugh - ter

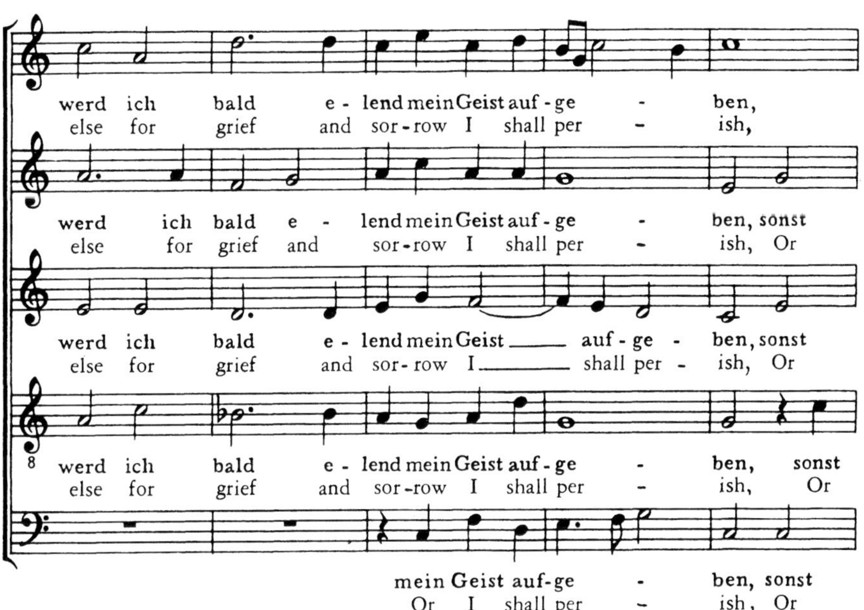
werd ich bald e - lend mein Geist auf-ge - ben,
else for grief and sor-row I shall per - ish,

werd ich bald e - lend mein Geist auf-ge - ben, sonst
else for grief and sor-row I shall per - ish, Or

werd ich bald e - lend mein Geist auf-ge - ben, sonst
else for grief and sor-row I shall per - ish, Or

werd ich bald e - lend mein Geist auf-ge - ben, sonst
else for grief and sor-row I shall per - ish, Or

mein Geist auf-ge - ben, sonst
Or I shall per - ish, Or

mein Geist auf - ge - ben.
Or I shall per - ish.

werd ich bald e - lend mein Geist auf - ge - ben.
else for grief and sor- row I shall per - ish.

werd ich bald e - lend mein Geist auf - ge - ben.
else for grief and sor - row I shall per - ish.

werd ich bald e - lend mein Geist auf - ge - ben.
else for grief and sor- row I shall per - ish.

werd ich bald e - lend mein Geist auf - ge - ben.
else for grief and sor- row I shall per - ish.

# In Bitter Woe and Anguish

Horatio Vecchi
1550-1605

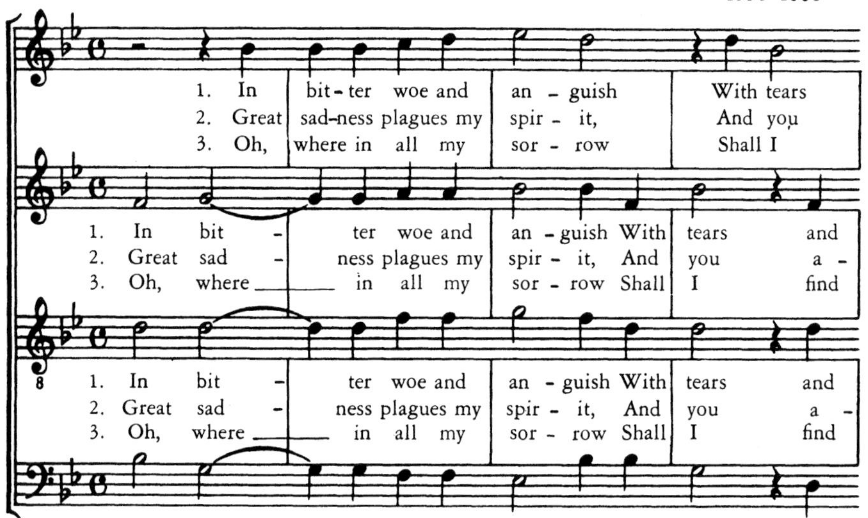


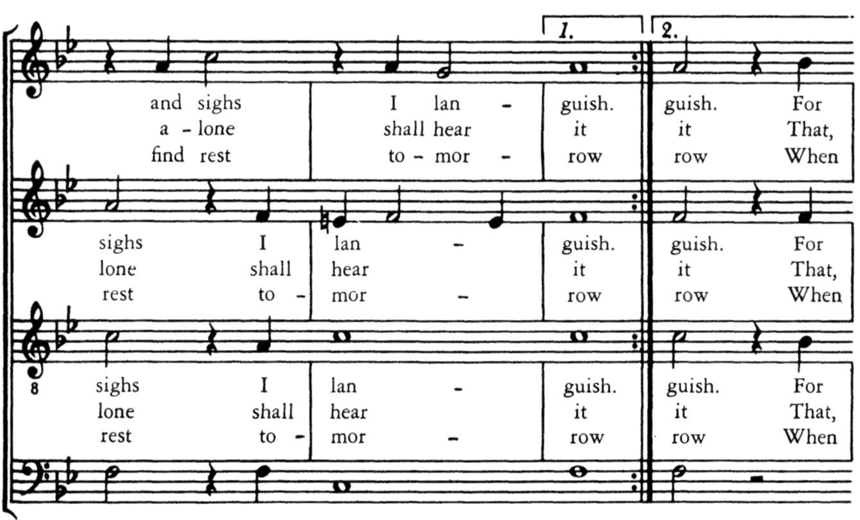

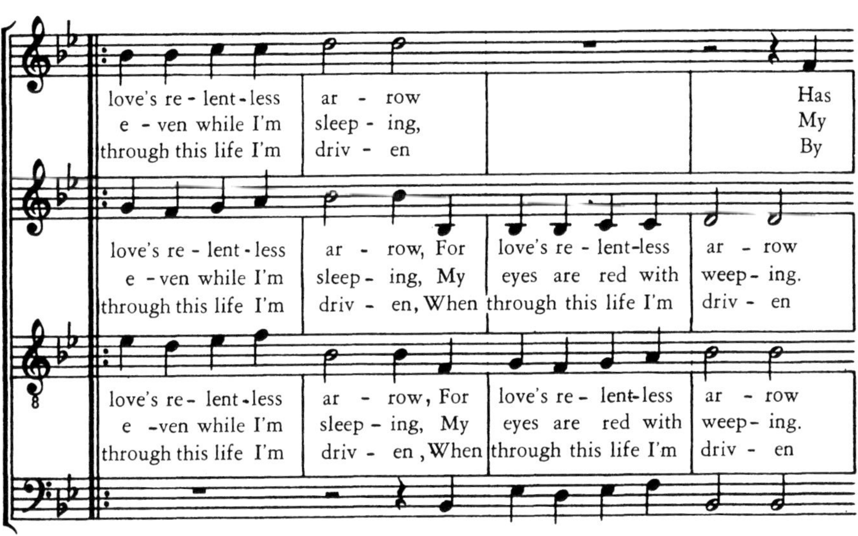
love's re - lent - less
e - ven while I'm
through this life I'm

ar - row
sleep - ing,
driv - en

Has
My
By

love's re - lent - less
e - ven while I'm
through this life I'm

ar - row, For
sleep - ing, My
driv - en, When

love's re - lent - less
eyes are red with
through this life I'm

ar - row
weep - ing.
driv - en

love's re - lent - less
e - ven while I'm
through this life I'm

ar - row, For
sleep - ing, My
driv - en, When

love's re - lent - less
eyes are red with
through this life I'm

ar - row
weep - ing.
driv - en

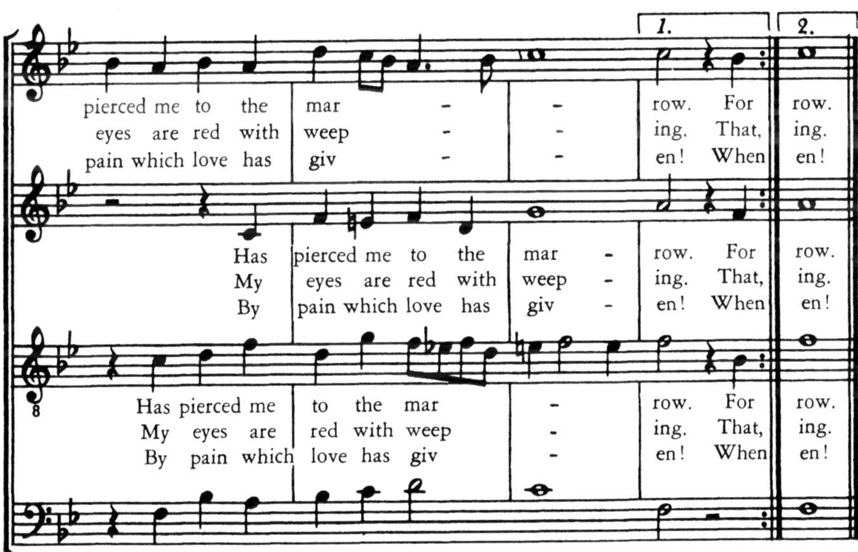
pierced me to the
eyes are red with
pain which love has

mar
weep
giv

row. For
ing. That,
en! When

row.
ing.
en!

Has
My
By

pierced me to the
eyes are red with
pain which love has

mar
weep
giv

row. For
ing. That,
en! When

row.
ing.
en!

Has pierced me
My eyes are
By pain which

to the mar
red with weep
love has giv

row. For
ing. That,
en! When

row.
ing.
en!

Wie weh tut mir mein Scheiden
My Love, I'm Filled With Sorrow

Melchior Franck
ca. 1573-1639

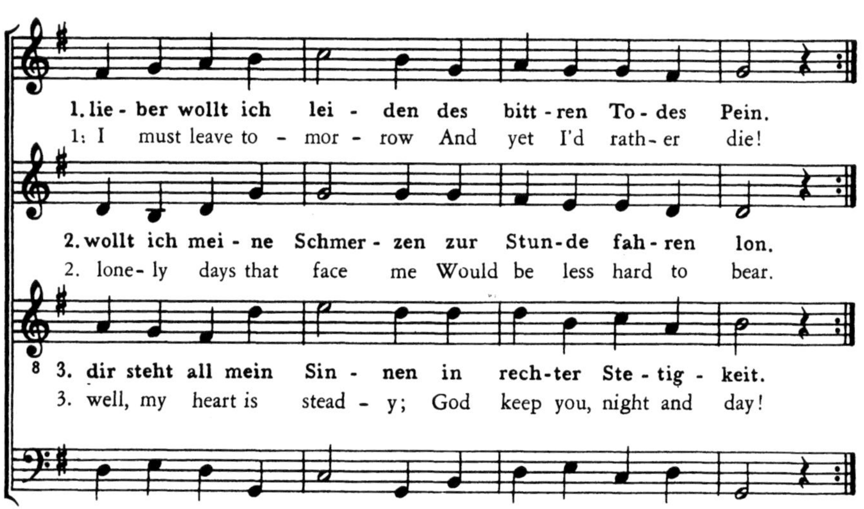

1.-3. Du tust al - lein das Her - ze mein freund -
When I am far From where you are Nor
1.-3. Du tust al - lein das Her - ze mein freund -
When I am far From where you are Nor
1.-3. Du tust al - lein das Her - ze mein freund -
When I am far From where you are Nor
lich in Lieb er - freun, dein und mein Treu sind
sun nor moon does shine. My love for you Is
lich in Lieb er - freun, dein und mein Treu sind
sun nor moon does shine. My love for you Is
lich in Lieb er - freun, dein und mein Treu sind
sun nor moon does shine. My love for you Is
täg - lich neu: Herz - lieb ich blei - be dein.
ev - er new. Oh, say that you are mine!
täg - lich neu: Herz - lieb ich blei - be dein.
ev - er new. Oh, say that you are mine!
täg - lich neu: Herz - lieb ich blei - be dein.
ev - er new. Oh, say that you are mine!

# Ich weiss mir ein Maidlein
## I Know a Young Lady

Orlando di Lasso
1532-1594

dich, es kann wohl falsch und freundlich sein,
ware! She'll play you false, so do take care!

dich, es kann wohl falsch und freundlich sein, es
ware! She'll play you false, so do take care! She'll

dich, es kann wohl falsch und freundlich sein, es
ware! She'll play you false, so do take care! She'll

dich, es
ware! She'll

hüt du dich, hüt du dich,
Do be -ware! Do be -ware!

kann wohl falsch und freundlich sein, hüt du dich, hüt du
play you false, so do take care! Do be - ware! Do be -

kann wohl falsch und freundlich sein, hüt du dich, hüt du
play you false, so do take care! Do be - ware! Do be -

kann wohl falsch und freundlich sein, hüt du dich, hüt du
play you false, so do take care! Do be - ware! Do be -

hüt du dich, ver-trau ihr nicht, hüt du dich, ver-trau ihr
Fair she is, but nev - er true: Fair she is, but nev - er

dich, hüt du dich, ver-trau ihr nicht, hüt du dich, ver-trau ihr
ware! Fair she is, but nev - er true: Fair she is, but nev - er

dich, hüt du dich, ver-trau ihr nicht, hüt du dich, ver-trau ihr
ware! Fair she is, but nev - er true: Fair she is, but nev - er

dich, hüt du dich, ver-trau ihr nicht, hüt du dich, ver-trau ihr
ware! Fair she is, but nev - er true: Fair she is, but nev - er

nicht, hüt du dich, ver - trau ihr nicht, sie nar-nar-nar- nar-
true: Fair she is, but nev - er true: She'll foo- foo- foo- foo-

nicht, hüt du dich, ver - trau ihr nicht, sie nar -nar-nar- nar-
true: Fair she is, but nev – er true: She'll foo- foo- foo- foo-

nicht, hüt du dich, ver - trau ihr nicht, sie nar-nar-nar- nar-
true: Fair she is, but nev - er true: She'll foo- foo- foo- foo-

nicht, hüt du dich, ver - trau ihr nicht, sie nar-nar-nar- nar-
true: Fair she is, but nev - er true: She'll foo- foo- foo- foo-

nar - ret dich, sie nar-nar-nar-nar - nar - ret
fool _____ you, too! She'll foo-foo- foo- foo- fool _____ you,

nar - ret dich, sie nar-nar-nar-nar nar - ret
fool _____ you, too! She'll foo-foo- foo- foo- fool _____ you,

nar - ret dich, sie nar-nar-nar-nar - nar - ret
fool you, too! She'll foo-foo- foo- foo- fool _____ you,

nar - ret dich, sie nar-nar-nar-nar - nar - ret
fool you, too! She'll foo-foo-foo- foo- fool _____ you,

1.
dich, hüt du dich,
too. Fair she is,
2.
dich, sie nar-nar-nar-nar- nar - ret dich.
too! She'll foo-foo-foo-foo- fool you, too.

dich, hüt du dich,
too. Fair she is,
dich, sie nar-nar-nar-nar - nar-nar-nar-ret dich.
too! She'll foo-foo-foo-foo- foo- foo- fool you, too.

dich, hüt du dich,
too. Fair she is,
dich, sie nar-nar-nar-nar - nar-nar-nar-ret dich.
too! She'll foo-foo-foo-foo- foo- foo- fool you, too.

dich, hüt du dich,
too. Fair she is,
dich, sie nar-nar-nar-nar - nar - ret dich.
too! She'll foo-foo-foo-foo- fool _____ you, too.

# Contents

by Composer

# Index

## by Title